Stopwatch books in hardback

Apple tree
Butterfly and caterpillar
Chicken and egg
Conker
Dandelion
Dragonfly
Earwig
Fly
Honeybee
House mouse

Ladybird
Mosquito
Moth
Mushroom
Newt
Potato
Stickleback
Strawberry
Tadpole and frog
Tomato

First paperback edition 1991

Reprinted 1994

First published 1986 in hardback by
A & C Black (Publishers) Limited
35 Bedford Row, London WC1R 4JH

ISBN 0-7136-3494-4

A CIP catalogue record for this book
is available from the British Library.

Acknowledgements
The artwork is by Helen Senior
The publishers would like to thank Jean Imrie for her help and advice.

Filmset by August Filmsetting, Haydock, St Helens
Printed in Belgium by Proost International Book Production

Birds' nest

Barrie Watts

A & C Black · London

Here is a blue tit.

Have you ever seen a blue tit? They live in parks and gardens. In summer they eat caterpillars and insects. In winter they might come to your bird table for scraps of food.

This blue tit is eating peanuts at a bird table.

Soon the blue tit will find a mate. When spring comes, they will both look for a place to build a nest and have their young.

This book will tell you how a blue tit family grows up.

The blue tits look for a place to build a nest.

The blue tits must find a safe dry place to build their nest. Some blue tits make their nests in holes in trees or walls. These birds have found a nesting box in someone's garden.

Look at the photograph. The female blue tit is looking inside the nesting box. The round hole is the only way to get in and out of the box. It will be a safe place to build a nest.

The blue tits build a nest.

The blue tits collect grass and moss to build their nest.
They carry it in their beaks back to the nesting box.
Then they arrange the grass into a nest.

Look at the big photograph. The female blue tit has
brought some hair and feathers to make the inside of
the nest soft and warm.

When the nest is finished, the blue tits will mate.

The female lays her eggs.

The female blue tit mates with the male many times.
Then she can start to lay her eggs. The eggs are very
small. Here is one next to a hen's egg.

Each morning, the female lays one egg. Then she flies
away. At night she comes back to the nest to sleep, and
the next day she lays another egg.

Look at the big photograph. How many eggs has the female
laid in her nest? Blue tits usually lay between seven and
fourteen eggs.

The blue tit keeps her eggs warm.

When the female blue tit has laid all her eggs, she sits on them to keep them warm. She keeps moving them round to make sure that each one is warm all over. If the eggs get cold they will not hatch.

The female blue tit has to sit on her eggs all day. She does not often fetch her own food. The male blue tit brings food to the nest for her.

The blue tits hatch out of the eggs.

After twelve days the birds hatch out of the eggs.
They are very hungry and they open their beaks wide
to ask for food.

These tiny birds are only one day old.

When the young birds hatch, they have no feathers and
cannot open their eyes. Each one is only as long as a pin.

Look at the big photograph. The young birds are now a
week old.

The young blue tits are always hungry.

Each young bird needs to eat over a hundred insects and caterpillars a day. The parent blue tits take it in turns to feed their young. Every few minutes they have to bring more food to the nest.

The young birds are now ten days old. They can open their eyes and they are beginning to grow feathers. First they grow quills, which are like short hard straws. You can see them in the photograph. Then feathers start to grow from the quills.

The blue tits keep their nest clean.

The blue tits must keep their nest clean. If it gets dirty the young birds could become ill.

Look at the photograph. The young blue tit is letting the male pull out its dropping.

The parent birds take away all the droppings and drop them on the ground away from the nest.

The young blue tits grow fast.

Now the young blue tits are fifteen days old.

Their eyes are wide open and they have grown soft grey and yellow feathers. They will not grow their adult feathers until the autumn.

The young blue tits are nearly as big as their mother and father. They still need to be fed by their parents.

The young birds get ready to leave the nest.

Soon the young birds start to explore the nesting box.
Look at the photograph. The blue tits are nineteen days old.
They are fully grown and soon they will leave the nest.

This young blue tit is stretching its wings. It is ready to fly.

The young blue tits learn how to fly.

On a warm sunny day, the blue tits fly out of the nest.
This young blue tit has just flown for the first time.
It is tired so it is having a rest on a branch.

The parent blue tits feed their young for three more
weeks. Then the young birds will have to find their own
food. They will leave their parents and fly away.

Next year the young blue tits will look for somewhere to
build a nest. What do you think will happen in the nest?

Do you remember what happens in a nest?
See if you can tell the story in your own words.
You can use these pictures to help you.

Index

This index will help you to find some of the important words in the book.

If you want blue tits to visit you, hang some unsalted peanuts outside in a string bag. Remember to put them in a safe sheltered place.